T0088227

love bites

food for thought and other
appetizing sentiments

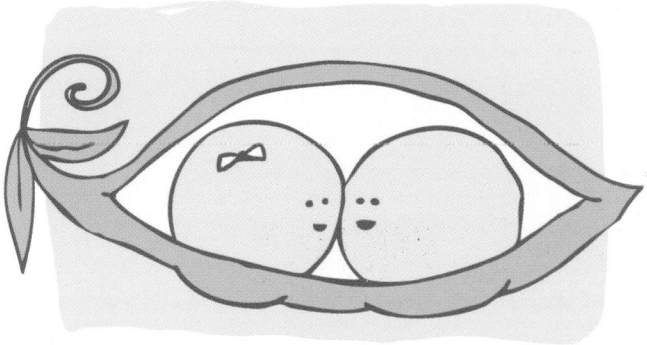

ben joel price

Skyhorse Publishing

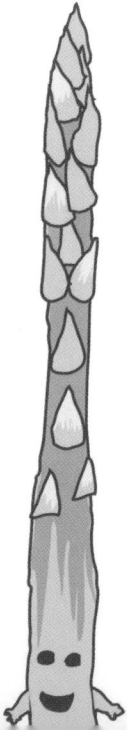

for all the lovers,
the foodies,
and the
foodie lovers...
enjoy!

'ello cupcake!

who's on top tonight then?

little pluckers

i love the hot tub; i'm so glad you finally fixed the bubble jets -
- fixed? Oh yeah... right ...

soapea

love chocolate

difference of opinion

you can be such a
little sweet heart! -

- it's 'cos i
love ya!

little gems

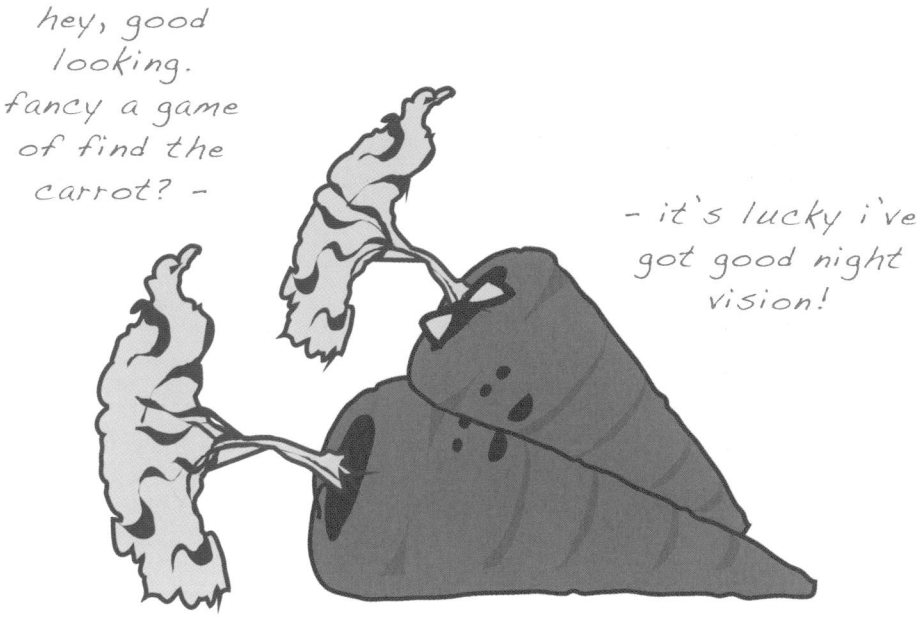
hey, good looking. fancy a game of find the carrot? -
- it's lucky i've got good night vision!

carrot top

little hotties

- oh, charming . . .
could you at least face me
when i'm talking to you?

- sulk

olive branch

Gaga or Minaj? -
- i have no idea what you just said...
Britney or Christina? -
- ahhh, i see

pop tarts!

- sigh!

check out the
birthday suit! -

the exhibitionist

prawn crackers

- it's not all been smooth sailing...

...but I'd swim to the end of the ocean for you

sole mates

spa tisane

hot and steamy

ménage a trios

-hey, Giusy, let's leave town and tie the knot

- that's a wonderful proposal, Walter, but i simply cantaloupe!

melons

first date

you make
me weak at
the knees,
hotcakes -

love stack, baby!

surprise! -

streaker

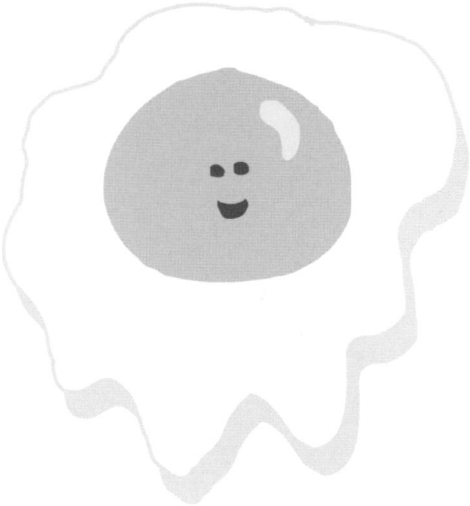

sunshine of my life

swirls just wanna have fun

ickle pickle giggle

- i`m hot,
i`m tasty,
i know how to salsa,
i`m filled with love,
i`m telling you, i`ll
spice up your
life forever!

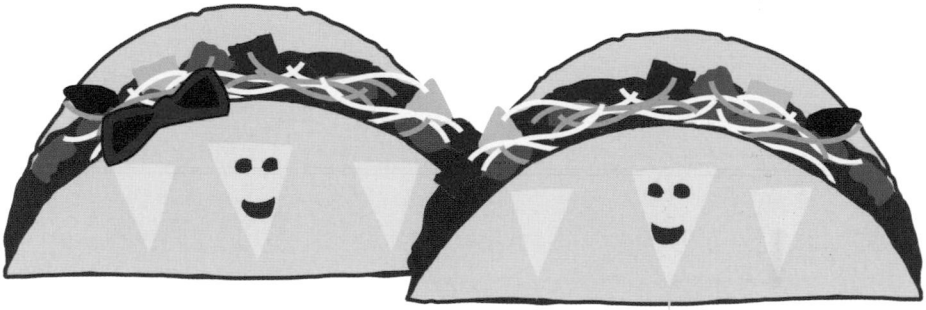

- look, stud,
let`s get one
thing straight, ok?
i`m nacho girl!

the hard shell

cocktail sausages

bad hair day

up beet

nacho man

- swoon

dough eyed

ooo, nice sprinkles, doughboy -

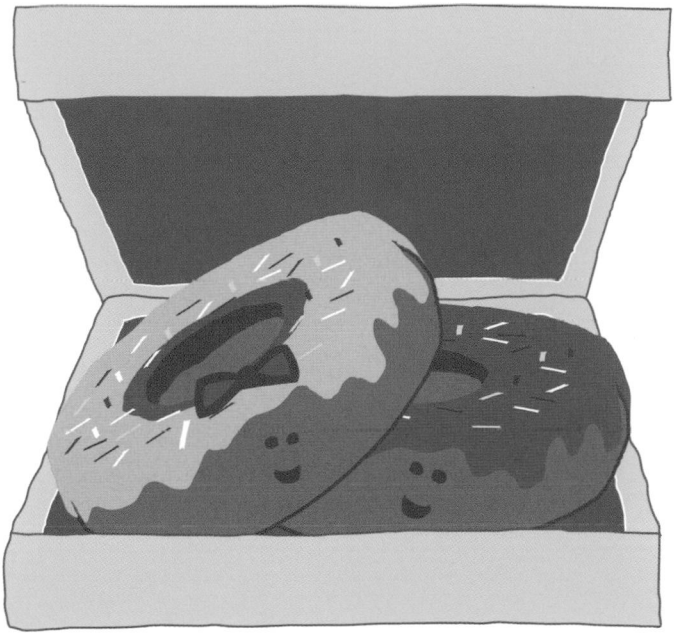

- oh, stick it in ya hole!

lovers glaze

fast food antics

salad dressing

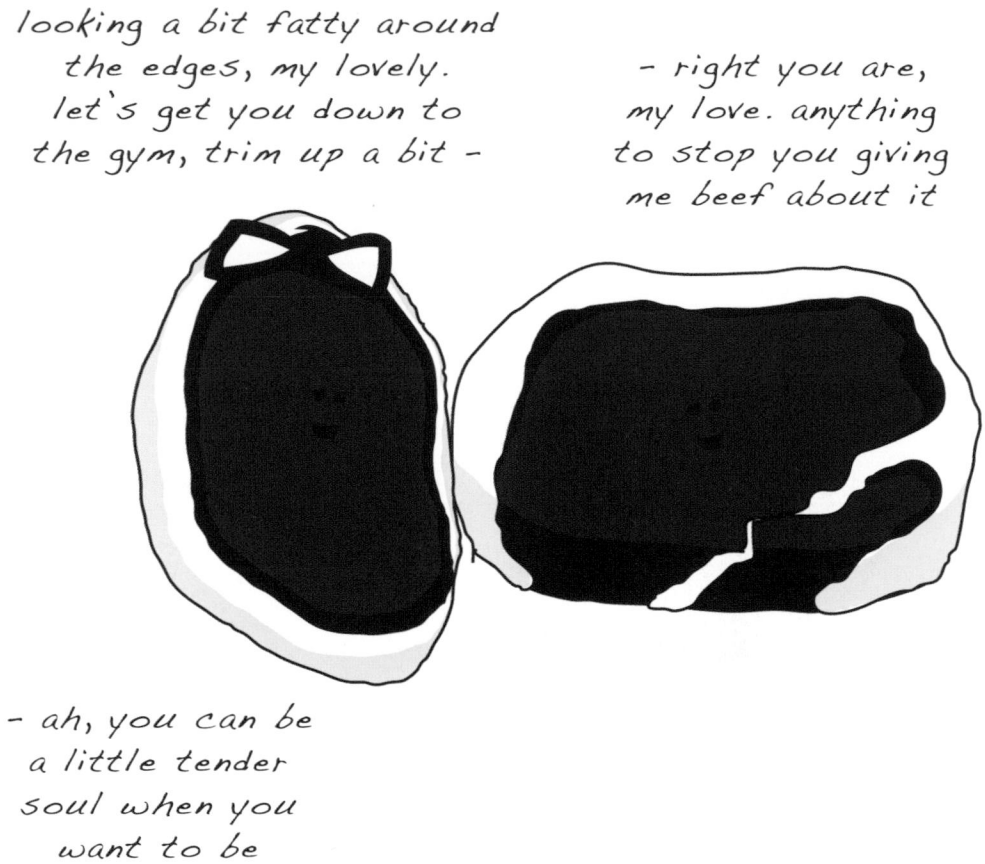
looking a bit fatty around the edges, my lovely. let's get you down to the gym, trim up a bit -
- right you are, my love. anything to stop you giving me beef about it
- ah, you can be a little tender soul when you want to be

food fight

shellfish lover

swingers

- out and proud! -

plums!

- she has that deep red complexion, but has "perfect skin" apparently. in my opinion, she's vinegar dressed as wine

- jealous much?

- i'm just saying... and i heard she's seedless, too!

sour grapes

um, honey, i don't want to
alarm you, but...
i think it's stuck! -

- oh, quit your drizzling

a sticky situation

this film is so corny -
- while i usually value your film critique, my sweet, right now a little hush time is required as i intend to spend the rest of my date with Ryan Gosling uninterrupted!

pop off

- udon love me anymore!

- oh, soba up, hun,
you know i love you oodles!

charmin' ramen

perfect catch

- hello, boys!

pin up

- hey, it's not the
size that counts...

self-assured

you're so mushy -

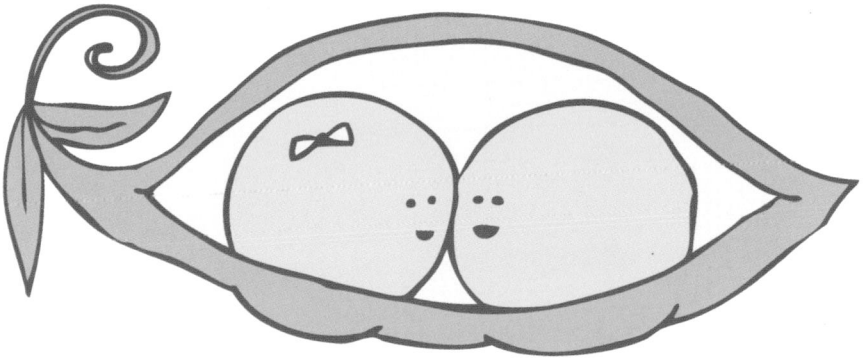

- give us a smooch

sweet pea

mac and roni,
"couple of the year, 2014,"
celebrating the best years spent
in comfort and sauce

so cheesy

- best legs in town!

- lickin' good, chick!

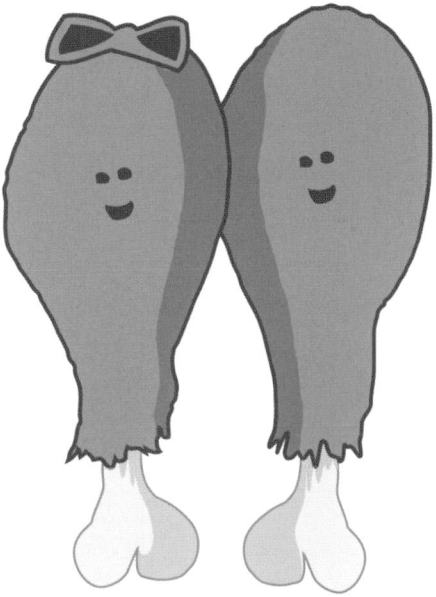

poulet vous?

- sob!

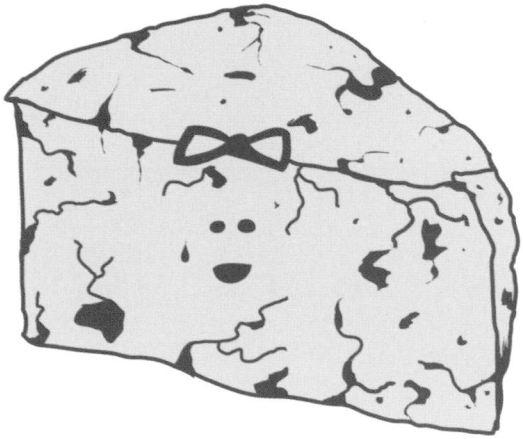

blue cheese

morning breath

premature mastication

run of the mill

apple of my eye

- you're always on my mind, sweetie

big softee

oops! i'm coming out at the sides -

- if you go on a diet, you know what they'll say: here today, cone tomorrow, ha!

groan. you can be so flaky at times -

coneheads

mixed feelings

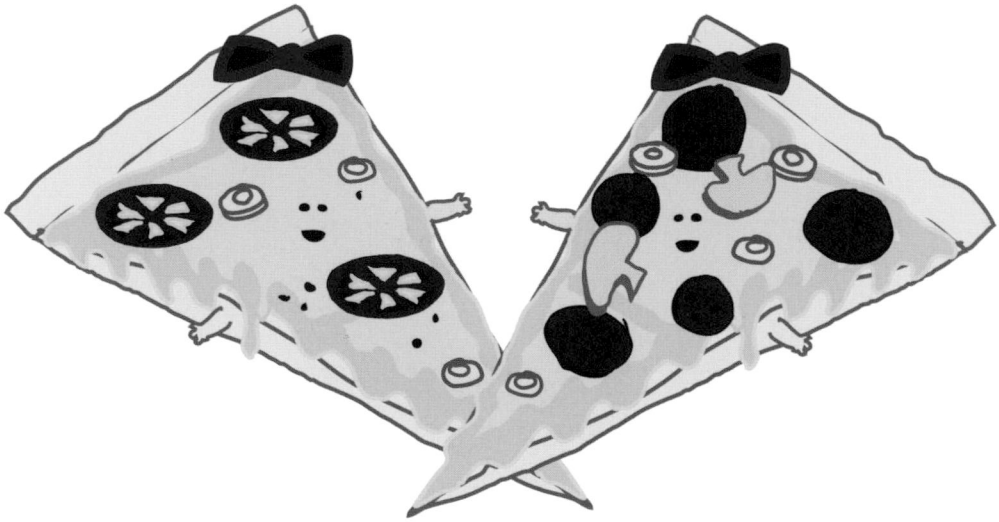

deep pan humor

nice pear

i'm gonna stick
with you forever,
sugar -

- sounds a
little hard
to swallow

gum love

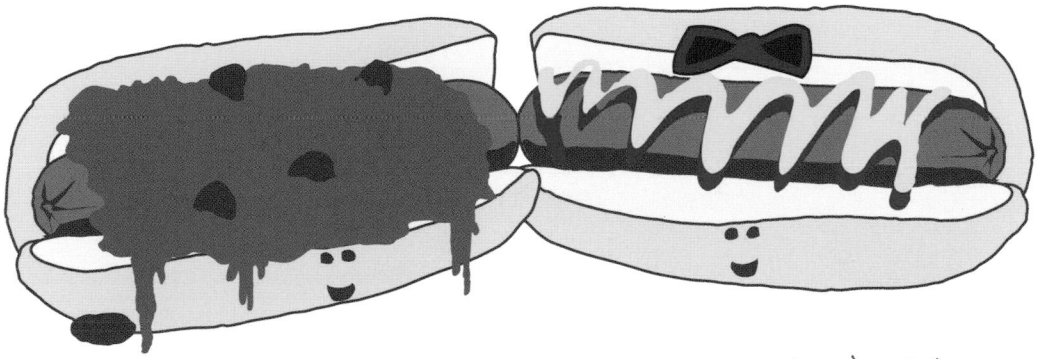
hey, saucy, i'm a bit chili. mind if i snuggle up between ya buns? -
- geesh! it's like living with a dog in heat!

down boy!

bride and legume

she loves you... -

-...he love-shallots!

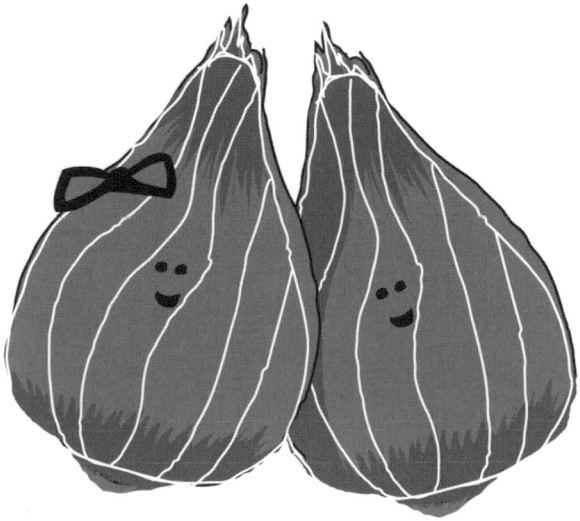

that shallot!

Acknowledgments

Yummy, yummy, yummy, I've got love in my tummy, and I feel like thanking you . . .
Nattles—my brilliant pea with whom I share my pod (told you . . . bit of asparagus!);
my parents—for providing the template for passion and pabulum;
Jan, Nan, Julita, Mr. Hobby, Isabel, and Julie for the sustenance and support;
and finally to food, which I simply couldn't live without.

Still hungry? Continue to spread the love and share a thought with a love bites greeting card available from: www.symetria.co.uk.

Copyright © 2014 by Ben Joel Price

All Rights Reserved. No part of this book may be reproduced in any manner without the express written consent of the publisher, except in the case of brief excerpts in critical reviews or articles. All inquiries should be addressed to Skyhorse Publishing, 307 West 36th Street, 11th Floor, New York, NY 10018.

Skyhorse Publishing books may be purchased in bulk at special discounts for sales promotion, corporate gifts, fund-raising, or educational purposes. Special editions can also be created to specifications. For details, contact the Special Sales Department, Skyhorse Publishing, 307 West 36th Street, 11th Floor, New York, NY 10018 or info@skyhorsepublishing.com.

Skyhorse® and Skyhorse Publishing® are registered trademarks of Skyhorse Publishing, Inc.®, a Delaware corporation.

Visit our website at www.skyhorsepublishing.com.

10 9 8 7 6 5 4 3 2 1

Library of Congress Cataloging-in-Publication Data is available on file.

ISBN: 978-1-62636-404-2

Printed in China